I0008551

CLOUD
COMPUTING

The Ultimate Beginners Guide

MANIPULATING,
CONFIGURING,
AND ACCESSING THE
APPLICATIONS ONLINE

i

CLOUD COMPUTING TUTORIAL

Cloud Computing provides us means by which we can access the applications as utilities over the internet. It allows us to create, configure, and customize the business applications online.

This tutorial will take you through a step-by-step approach while learning Cloud Computing concepts.

AUDIENCE

This reference has been prepared for the beginners to help them to understand basic-to-advanced concepts related to Cloud Computing. This tutorial will give you enough understanding on Cloud Computing concepts from where you can take yourself to a higher level of expertise.

PREREQUISITES

Before proceeding with this tutorial, you should have basic knowledge of Computers, Internet, Database and Networking concepts. Such basic knowledge will help you in understanding the Cloud Computing concepts and move fast on the learning track.

TABLE OF CONTENTS

WHAT IS CLOUD?

The term **Cloud** refers to a **Network** or **Internet**. In other words, we can say that Cloud is something which is present at remote location. Cloud can provide services over network i.e. on public networks or on private networks i.e. WAN, LAN or VPN.

Applications such as **e-mail, web conferencing, customer relationship management (CRM),** all run in cloud.

WHAT IS CLOUD COMPUTING?

Cloud Computing refers to **manipulating, configuring,** and **accessing** the applications online. It offers online data storage, infrastructure and application.

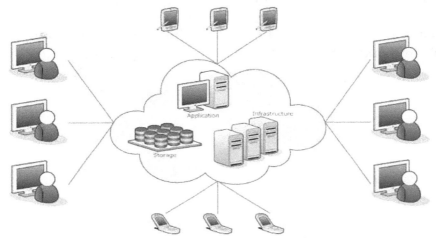

We need not to install a piece of software on our local PC and this is how, the cloud computing overcomes **platform dependency issues**. Hence, the Cloud Computing is making our business application **mobile**and **collaborative**.

CLOUD COMPUTING TECHNOLOGIES

There are certain technologies that are working behind the cloud computing platforms making cloud computing flexible, reliable, usable. These technologies are listed below:

- Virtualization
- Service-Oriented Architecture (SOA)
- Grid Computing
- Utility Computing

VIRTUALIZATION

Virtualization is a technique which allows to share single physical instance of an application or resource among multiple organizations or tenants(customers). It does so by assigning a logical name to a physical resource and providing a pointer to that physical resource when demanded.

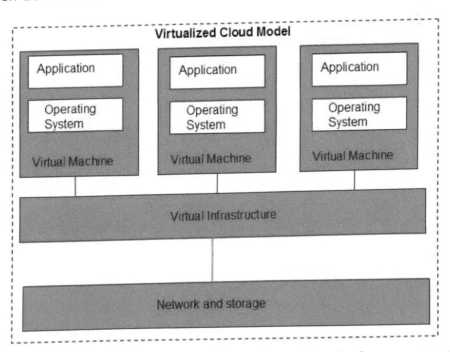

The **Multitenant** architecture offers **virtual isolation** among the multiple tenants and therefore, the organizations can use and customize the application as though, they each has its own instance running.

SERVICE-ORIENTED ARCHITECTURE(SOA)

Service-Oriented Architecture helps to use applications as a service for other applications regardless type of vendor, product or technology. Therefore it is possible to exchange of data between applications of different vendors without additional programming or making changes to services.

cloud_computing-service_oriented_architecture

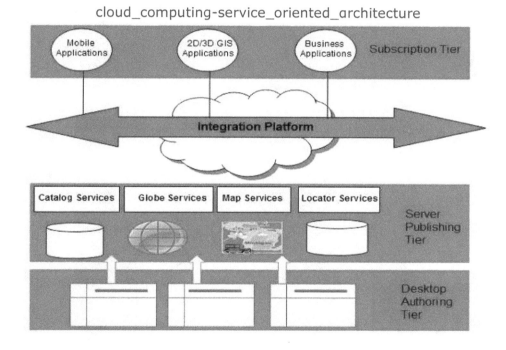

GRID COMPUTING

Grid Computing refers to distributed computing in which a group computers from multiple locations are connected with each other to achieve common objective. These computer resources are heterogeneous and geographically dispersed.

Grid Computing breaks complex task into smaller pieces. These smaller pieces are distributed to CPUs that reside within the grid.

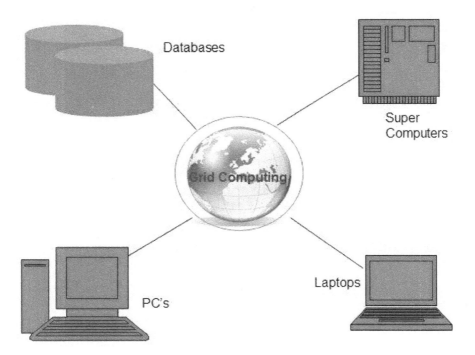

UTILITY COMPUTING

Utility computing is based on **Pay per Use** model. It offers computational resources on demand as a metered service. Cloud computing, grid computing, and managed IT services are based on the concept of Utility computing.

CLOUD COMPUTING ARCHITECTURE

The Cloud Computing architecture comprises of many cloud components, each of them are loosely coupled. we can broadly divide the cloud architecture into two parts:

- Front End
- Back End

Each of the ends are connected through a network, usually via. Internet. The following diagram shows the graphical view of cloud computing architecture:

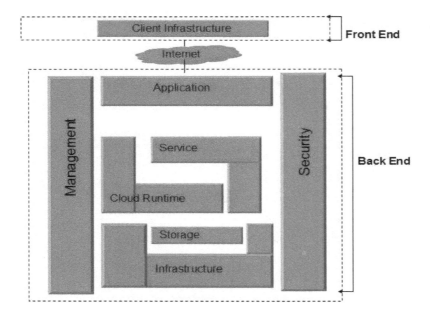

8

FRONT END

Front End refers to the client part of cloud computing system. It consist of interfaces and applications that are required to access the cloud computing platforms. Eg. Web Browser

BACK END

Back End refers to the cloud itself. It consist of all the resources required to provide cloud computing services. It comprises of huge **data storage, virtual machines, security mechanism, services, deployment models, servers**etc.

CLOUD INFRASTRUCTURE COMPONENTS

Cloud infrastructure consist of servers, storage, network, management software, and deployment software and platform virtualization.

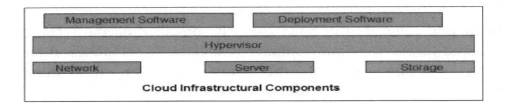

Cloud Infrastructural Components

HYPERVISOR

Hypervisor is a **firmware** or **low level program** that acts as a Virtual Machine Manager. It allows to share the single physical instance of cloud resources between several tenants.

MANAGEMENT SOFTWARE

Management Software helps to maintain and configure the infrastructure.

DEPLOYMENT SOFTWARE

Deployment software helps to deploy and integrate the application on the cloud.

NETWORK

Network is the key component of cloud infrastructure. It allows to connect cloud services over the internet. It is also possible to deliver network as a utility over the internet i.e. the consumer can customize the network route and protocol.

SERVER

Server helps to compute the resource sharing and offer other services such as resource allocation and de allocation, monitoring resources, security etc.

STORAGE

Cloud uses distributed file system for storage purpose. If one of the storage resource fails then it can be extracted from another one, which makes cloud computing more reliable.

CLOUD DEPLOYMENT MODELS

Foloowing are the cloud deployment models:

- Public Cloud Model
- Private Cloud Model
- Hybrid Cloud Model
- Community Cloud Model

PUBLIC CLOUD MODEL

The **Public Cloud Model** allows systems and services to be easily accessible to general public. e.g. **Google, Amazon, Microsoft** offers cloud services via internet.

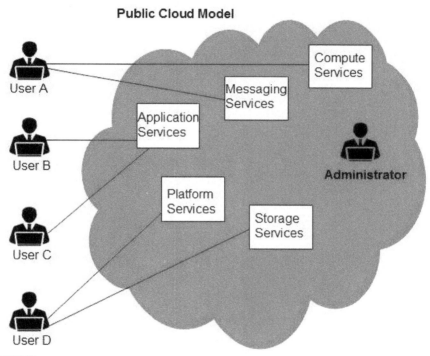

Public Cloud Model

BENEFITS

- Cost Effective
- Reliability
- Flexibility
- Location Independence
- Utility Style Costing
- High Scalability

DISADVANTAGES
- Low Security
- Less customizable

PRIVATE CLOUD MODEL

The **Private Cloud** allows systems and services to be accessible with in an organization. The Private Cloud is operated only within a single organization. However, It may be managed internally or by third-party.

Private Cloud Model

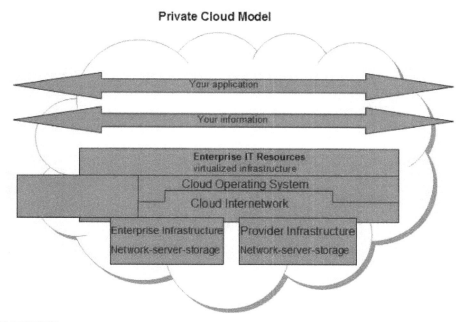

BENEFITS

Here are the benefits of deploying cloud as private cloud model.

- Higher Security and Privacy
- More Control
- Cost and energy efficiency

DISADVANTAGES

Here are the disadvantages of using private cloud model:

15

- Restricted Area
- Inflexible Pricing
- Limited Scalability
- Additional Skills

HYBRID CLOUD MODEL

The **Hybrid Cloud** is mixture of **public** and **private** cloud. Non Critical activities are performed using public cloud while the critical activities are performed using private cloud.

BENEFITS

Here are the benefits of deploying cloud as hybrid cloud model:

- Scalability
- Flexibility
- Cost Efficiencies

DISADVANTAGES

Here are the disadvantages of Hybrid Cloud Model:

- Networking Issues
- Security Compliance
- Infrastructural Dependency

COMMUNITY CLOUD MODEL

The **Community Cloud** allows system and services to be accessible by group of organizations. It shares the infrastructure between several organizations from a specific community. It may be managed internally or by the third-party.

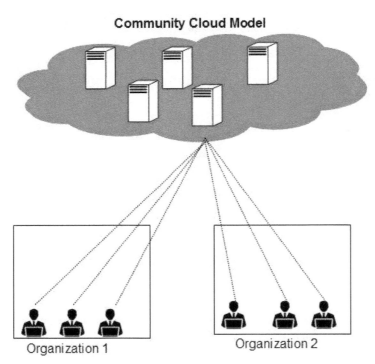

Community Cloud Model

Organization 1   Organization 2

BENEFITS

Here are the benefits of deploying cloud as **community cloud model**:

- Cost effective
- Sharing Between Organizations
- Security

ISSUES

- Since all data is housed at one location, therefore one must be careful in storing data in community cloud because it might be accessible by others.
- It is also challenging to allocate responsibilities of governance, security and cost.

CLOUD SERVICE MODELS

Following are the cloud service models:

- Infrastructure as a Service(IaaS) Model
- Platform as a Service(PaaS) Model
- Software as a Service(SaaS) Model
- Identity as a Service(IDaaS) Model
- Network as a Service(NaaS) Model

INFRASTRUCTURE AS A SERVICE(IaaS)

IaaS provides access to fundamental resources such as physical machines, virtual machines, virtual storage etc. Apart from these resource the IaaS also offers:

- Virtual machine disk storage
- Virtual local area network (VLANs)
- Load balancers
- IP addresses
- Software bundles

All of the above resources are made available to end user via **server virtualization**. Moreover, these resources are accessed by the customers as if they own them.

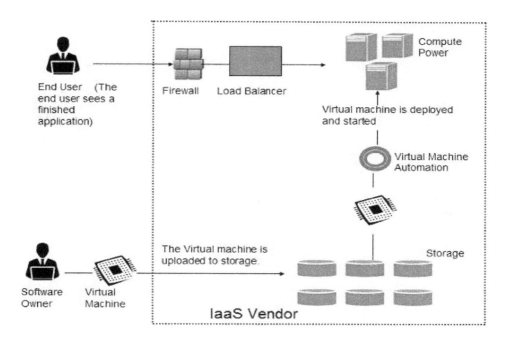

BENEFITS

IaaS allows the cloud provider to freely locate the infrastructure over the internet in cost-effective manner. Some of the key benefits of IaaS are listed below:

- Full Control of the computing resources through Administrative Access to VMs.
- Flexible and Efficient renting of Computer Hardware.
- Portability, Interoperability with Legacy Applications.

ISSUES

Here are the issues associated with IaaS:

- Compatibility with Legacy Security Vulnerabilities
- Virtual Machine Sprawl
- Robustness of VM-level Isolation
- Data Erase Practices

CHARACTERISTICS

Here are the characteristics of IaaS service model:

- Virtual machines with pre-installed software.
- Virtual machines with pre-installed Operating Systems such as windows, Linux, and Solaris.
- On-demand availability of resources.
- Allows to store copies of particular data in different locations.
- The computing resources can be easily scaled up and down.

PLATFORM AS A SERVICE(PAAS)

PaaS offers the run time environment for applications. It also offers development & deployment tools, required to develop applications. PaaS has a feature of **point-and-click** tools that enables non-developers to create web applications.

The following diagram shows how PaaS offers an API and development tools to the developers and how it helps the end user to access business applications.

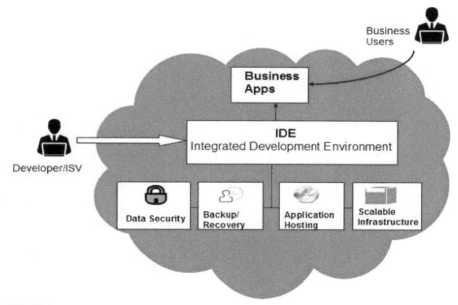

BENEFITS
Following are the benefits of PaaS model:

- Lower administrative overhead
- Lower total cost of ownership
- Scalable Solutions

- More current system software

ISSUES

Like **SaaS**, **PaaS** also place significant burdens on consumer's browsers to maintain reliable and secure connections to the provider systems. Therefore, PaaS shares many of the issues of SaaS. However, there are some specific issues associated with PaaS as listed below:

- Lack of portability between PaaS clouds
- Event Based Processor Scheduling
- Security Engineering of PaaS applications

Software as a Service (SaaS)

Software as a Service(SaaS) model allows to provide software applications as a service to the end users. It refers to a software that is deployed on a hosted service and is accessible via internet. There are several SaaS applications. Some of them are listed below:

- Billing and Invoicing System
- Customer Relationship Management (CRM) applications
- Help Desk Applications
- Human Resource (HR) Solutions

CHARACTERISTICS

Here are the characteristics of SaaS service model:

- SaaS makes the software available over the internet.
- The Software are maintained by the vendor rather than where they are running.
- The license to the software may be subscription based or usage based. And it is billed on recurring basis.
- SaaS applications are cost effective since they do not require any maintenance at end user side.
- They are available on demand.
- They can be scaled up or down on demand.
- They are automatically upgraded and updated.
- SaaS offers share data model. Therefore multiple users can share single instance of infrastructure. It is not required to hard code the functionality for individual users.
- All users are running same version of the software.

BENEFITS

Using SaaS has proved to be beneficial in term of scalability, efficiency, performance and much more. Some of the benefits are listed below:

- Modest Software Tools
- Efficient use of Software Licenses
- Centralized Management & Data
- Platfrom responsibilities managed by provider
- Multitenant solutions.

ISSUES

There are several issues associated with SaaS. Some of them are listed below:

- Browser based risks
- Network dependence
- Lack of portability between SaaS clouds

IDENTITY AS A SERVICE(IDaaS)

Employees in a company require to login to system to perform various tasks. These systems may be based on local server or cloud based. Following are the problems that an employee might face:

- Remembering different username and password combinations for accessing multiple servers.
- If an employee leaves the company, It's required to ensure that each of the user's account has been disabled. This increases workload on IT staff.

To solve above problems, a new technique emerged which is known as **Identity as a Service (IDaaS)**.

IDaaS offers management of identity (information) as a digital entity. This identity can be used during electronic transactions.

Identity refers to set of attributes associated with something and make it recognizable. All objects may have some same attributes but their identity can not be the same. This unique identity is assigned through unique identification attribute.

There are several **identity services** that have been deployed to validate services such as validating web sites, transactions, transaction participants, client etc. Identity as a Service may include the following:
- Directory Services
- Federated Services
- Registration
- Authentication Services
- Risk and Event monitoring
- Single sign-on services
- Identity and Profile management

SINGLE SIGN-ON (SSO)

To solve the problem of using different username & password combination for different servers, companies now employ Single Sign-On software, which allows the user to login only one time and manages the user's access to other systems.

SSO has single authentication server, managing multiple access to other systems, as shown in the following diagram:

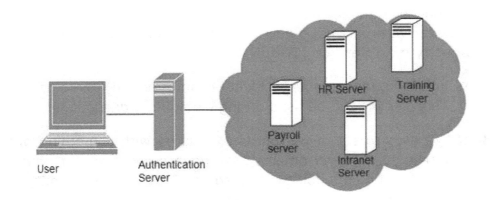

SSO WORKING

There are several implementations of SSO. Here, we discuss the common working of SSO:

28

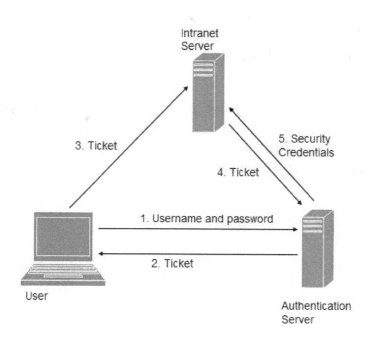

Following steps explain the working of Single Sign-On software:

1. User logs into the authentication server using a username and password.
2. The authentication server returns the user's ticket.
3. User sends the ticket to intranet server.
4. Intranet server sends the ticket to the authentication server.
5. Authentication server sends the user's security credentials for that server back to the intranet server.

If an employee leaves the company, then it just required to disable the user at the authentication server, which in turn disable the user's access to all the systems.

FEDERATED IDENTITY MANAGEMENT(FIDM)

FIDM describes the technologies and protocols that enable a user to package security credentials across security domains. It uses **Security Markup Language (SAML)** to package a user's security credentials as shown in the following diagram:

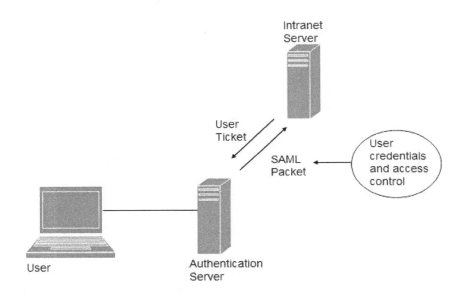

OPENID

It offers users to login multiple websites with single account. Google, Yahoo!, Flickr, MySpace, WordPress.com are some of the companies that support OpenID.

BENEFITS

- Increased site conversation rates.
- Access to greater user profile content.
- Fewer problems with lost passwords.
- Ease of content integration into social networking sites.

Network as a Service(NaaS)

OVERVIEW

Networks as a Service allows us to access to network infrastructure directly and securely. NaaS makes it possible to deploy **custom routing protocols**.

NaaS uses **virtualized network infrastructure** to provide network services to the consumer. It is the responsibility of NaaS provider to maintain and manage the network resources, which decreases the workload from the consumer. Moreover, NaaS offers **network as a utility**.

NaaS is also based on **pay-per-use** model.

HOW NAAS IS DELIVERED?

To use NaaS model, the consumer is required to logon to the web portal, where he can get on line API. Here, the consumer can customize the route.

In turn, consumer has to pay for the capacity used. It is also possible to turn off the capacity at any time.

MOBILE NAAS

Mobile NaaS offers more efficient and flexible control over mobile devices. It uses virtualization to simplify the architecture to create more efficient processes.

Following diagram shows the Mobile NaaS service elements:

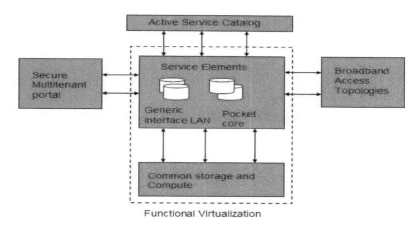

Functional Virtualization

NAAS BENEFITS

NaaS offers a number of benefits, some of the are discussed below:

- Independence
- Analytics
- Resilience
- Ease of Adding new Service Elements
- Isolation of customer traffic
- Support Models

CLOUD MANAGEMENT TASKS

Cloud Management involves a number of tasks to be performed by the cloud provider to ensure efficient use of cloud resources. Here, we will discuss some of these tasks:

- Audit System Backups
- System's Data Flow Management
- Ensuring no Vendor Lock-in
- Provider's security procedures
- Monitor Capacity Planning and Scaling Capabilities
- Monitor Audit-Log Use
- Solution testing and Validation

CLOUD DATA STORAGE

Cloud Storage is a service that allows to save data on offsite storage system managed by third party and is made accessible by a **web services API**.

STORAGE DEVICES

Storage devices can be broadly classified into two categories:

- Block Storage Devices
- File Storage Devices

BLOCK STORAGE DEVICES

Block Storage Devices offers the raw storage to the clients. This raw storage can be partitioned to create volumes.

FILE STORAGE DEVICES

File Storage Devices offers storage to clients in form of files, maintaining its own file system. This storage is in the form of Network Attached Storage (NAS).

CLOUD STORAGE CLASSES

Cloud Storage can be broadly classified into two categories:

- Unmanaged Cloud Storage
- Managed Cloud Storage

UNMANAGED CLOUD STORAGE

Unmanaged Cloud Storage means that the storage is preconfigured for the consumer. The consumer can not format nor the consumer can install own file system or change drive properties.

MANAGED CLOUD STORAGE

Managed Cloud Storage offers online storage space on demand. Managed cloud storage system presents what appears to the user to be a raw disk that the user can partition and format.

CREATING CLOUD STORAGE SYSTEM

The cloud storage system stores multiple copes of data on multiple servers and in multiple locations. If one system fails then it only requires to change the pointer to stored object's location.

To aggregate storage assets into cloud storage systems, the cloud provider can use storage virtualization software, **StorageGRID**. It creates a virtualization layer that fetches storage from different storage devices into a single management system. It can also manage data from **CIFS** and **NFS** file system over the Internet. The following diagram shows how SystemGRID virtualizes the storage into storage clouds:

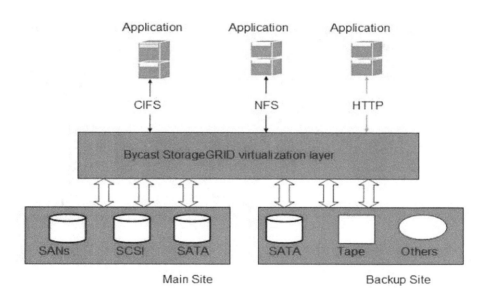

VIRTUAL STORAGE CONTAINERS

Virtual storage containers offer high performance cloud storage systems. **Logical Unit Number (LNU)** of device, files and other objects are created in virtual storage containers. Following diagram shows a virtual storage container, defining a cloud storage domain:

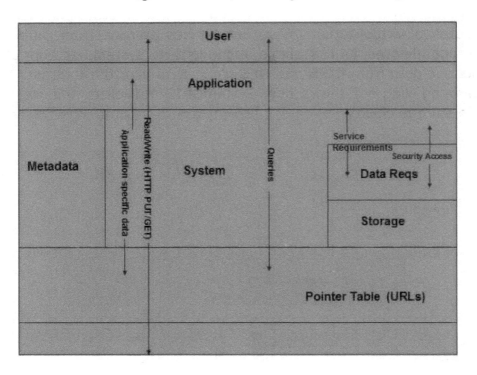

CHALLENGES

Storing the data in cloud is not that simple task. Apart from its flexibility and convenience, it also has several challenges faced by the consumers. The consumers require ability to:

- Provision additional storage on demand.
- Know and restrict the physical location of the stored data.
- Verify how data was erased?
- Have access to a documented process for surely disposing of data storage hardware.
- Administrator access control over data.

VIRTUALIZATION CONCEPT

Creating a virtual machine over existing operating system and hardware is referred as Hardware Virtualization. Virtual Machines provide an environment that is logically separated from the underlying hardware.

The machine on which the virtual machine is created is known as **host machine** and **virtual machine** is referred as a **guest machine**. This virtual machine is managed by a software or firmware which is known as **hypervisor**.

HYPERVISOR

Hypervisor is a firmware or low level program that acts as a Virtual Machine Manager. There are two types of hypervisor:

Type 1 hypervisor runs on bare system. **LynxSecure, RTS Hypervisor, Oracle VM, Sun xVM Server, VirtualLogic VLX** are examples of Type 1 hypervisor. The following diagram shows the Type 1 hypervisor.

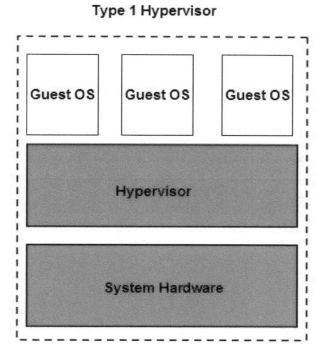

Type 1 Hypervisor

The **type1 hypervisor** does not have any host operating system because they are installed on a bare system.

Type 2 hypervisor is a software interface that emulates the devices with which a system normally interacts. **Containers, KVM,**

Microsoft Hyper V, VMWare Fusion, Virtual Server 2005 R2, Windows Virtual PC and **VMWare workstation 6.0** are examples of Type 2 hypervisor. The following diagram shows the Type 2 hypervisor.

Type 2 Hypervisor

Guest OS	Guest OS	Guest OS

Hypervisor

Host Operating System

TYPES OF HARDWARE VIRTUALIZATION

Here are the three types of hardware virtualization:

1. Full Virtualization
2. Emulation Virtualization
3. Paravirtualization

FULL VIRTUALIZATION

In **Full Virtualization**, the underlying hardware is completely simulated. Guest software do not require any modification to run.

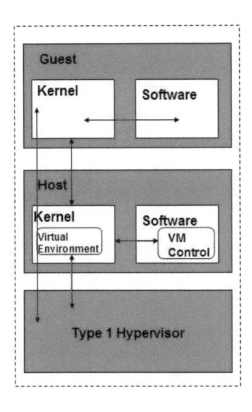

EMULATION VIRTUALIZATION

In **Emulation**, the virtual machine simulates the hardware and hence become independent of the it. In this, the guest operating system does not require modification.

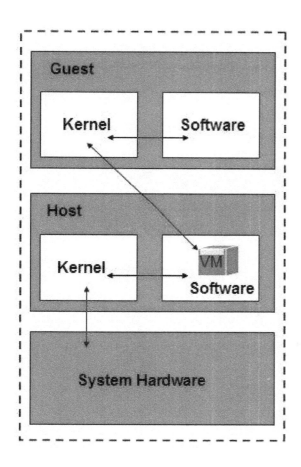

PARAVIRTUALIZATION

In **Paravirtualization**, the hardware is not simulated. The guest software run their own isolated domains.

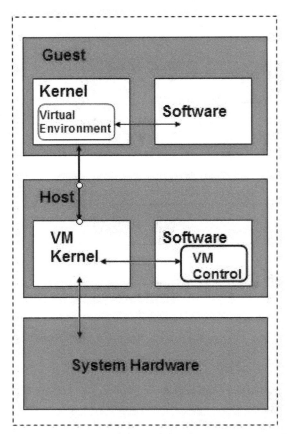

VMware vSphere is highly developed infrastructure that offers a management infrastructure framework for virtualization. It virtualizes the system, storage and networking hardware.

Securing the Cloud

Security in cloud computing is a major concern. Data in cloud should be stored in encrypted form. To restrict client from direct accessing the shared data, proxy and brokerage services should be employed.

Security Planning

Before deploying a particular resource to cloud, one should need to analyze several attributes about the resource such as:

- Select which resources, he is going to move to cloud and analyze its sensitivity to risk.
- Consider cloud service models such as **IaaS, PaaS**, and **SaaS**. These models require consumer to be responsible for security at different level of service.
- Consider which cloud type such as **public, private, community** or **hybrid**.
- Understand the cloud service provider's system that how data is transferred, where it is stored and how to move data into and out of cloud.

Mainly the risk in cloud deployment depends upon the service models and cloud types.

UNDERSTANDING SECURITY OF CLOUD SECURITY BOUNDARIES

A particular service model defines the boundary between the responsibilities of service provider and consumer. **Cloud Security Alliance (CSA)** stack model defines the boundaries between each service model and shows how different functional units relate to each other. The following diagram shows the **CSA stack model:**

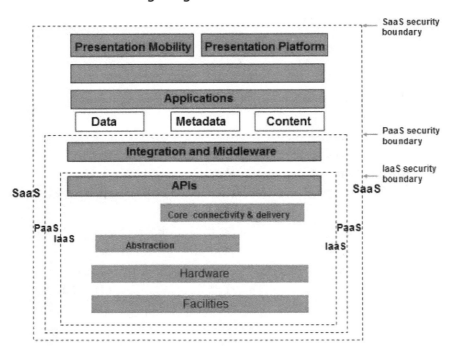

KEY POINTS TO CSA MODEL:

- IaaS is the most basic level of service with PaaS and SaaS next two above level of service.
- Moving upwards each of the service inherits capabilities and security concerns of the model beneath.
- IaaS provides the infrastructure, PaaS provides platfrom development environment and SaaS provides operating environment.
- IaaS has the least level of integrated functionalities and integrated security while SaaS has the most.
- This model describes the security boundaries at which cloud service provider's responsibility ends and the consumer's responsibilities begin.
- Any security mechanism below the security boundary must be built into the system and above should me maintained by the consumer.

Although each service model has security mechanism but security needs also depends upon where these services are located, in private, public, hybrid or community cloud.

UNDERSTANDING DATA SECURITY

Since all the data is transferred using internet, therefore, data security is of major concern in cloud. Here are key mechanisms for protecting data mechanisms listed below:

- Access Control
- Auditing
- Authentication
- Authorization

All of the service model must should incorporate security mechanism operating in all above mentioned areas.

Isolated Access to Data

Since data stored in the cloud can be accessed from anywhere, therefore, in order to protect the data, we must have a mechanism to protect it from the client direct access.

Brokered Cloud Storage Access is one of the approach for isolating the storage in cloud. In this approach two services are created:

- A broker with full access to storage but no access to client.
- A proxy with no access to storage but access to both client and broker.

WORKING OF BROKERED CLOUD STORAGE ACCESS SYSTEM

When the client issue request to access data:

- The client data request goes to proxy's external service interface.
- The proxy forwards the request to the broker.
- The broker requests the data from cloud storage system.
- The cloud storage system returns the data to the broker.
- The broker returns the data to proxy.
- Finally the proxy sends the data to the client.

All of the above steps are shown in the following diagram:

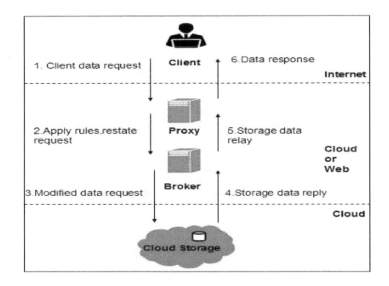

ENCRYPTION

Encryption helps to protect data from being compromised. It protects data that is being transferred as well as data stored in the cloud. Although encryption helps to protect data from any unauthorized access, it does not prevent from data loss.

CLOUD COMPUTING OPERATIONS OVERVIEW

Cloud computing operation refers to delivering superior cloud service. Today cloud computing operations have become very popular and widely employed by many of the organizations just because, it allows to perform all business operations over the internet.

These operations can be performed using a web application or mobile based applications. There are a number of operations that are performed in cloud, some of them are shown in the following diagram:

MANAGING CLOUD OPERATIONS

There are several ways to manage day to day cloud operations, as shown in the following diagram:

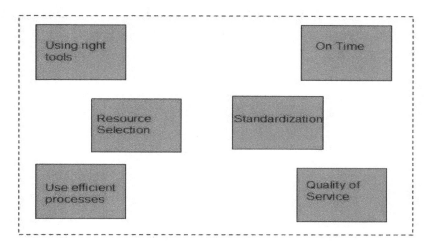

- Always employ right tools and resources to perform any function in the cloud.
- Things should be done at right time and at right cost.
- Selecting an appropriate resource is mandatory for operation management.
- The process should be standardized and automated to avoid repetitive tasks.
- Using efficient process will eliminate the waste and redundancy.
- One should maintain the quality of service to avoid re-work later.

CLOUD APPLICATIONS

Cloud Computing has its applications in almost all the fields such as **business, entertainment, data storage, social networking, management, entertainment, education, art** and **global positioning system** etc. Some of the widely famous cloud computing applications are discusses here in this tutorial:

BUSINESS APPLICATIONS

Cloud computing has made business more collaborative and easy by incorporating various apps such as **MailChimp, Chatter, Google Apps for business**, and **Quickbooks**.

SN	Application Description
1	**MailChimp** It offers an **email publishing platfrom.** It is widely employed by the businesses to design and send their email campaigns.
2	**Chatter** **Chatter app** helps the employee to share important information about organization in real time. One can get the instant feed regarding any issue.
3	**Google Apps for Business** **Google** offers **creating text documents, spreadsheets, presentations**etc. on **Google Docs** which allows the business users to share them in collaborating manner.
4	**Quickbooks** It offers **online accounting solutions** for a business. It helps in **monitoring cash flow, creating VAT returns** and **creating business reports**.

Data Storage and Backup

Box.com, Mozy, Joukuu are the applications, offering data storage and backup services in cloud.

SN	Application Description
1	**Box.com** **Box.com** offers drag and drop service for files. It just required to drop the files into Box and access from anywhere.
2	**Mozy** **Mozy** offers online backup service for files during a data loss.
3	**Joukuu** **Joukuu** is a web based interface. It allows to display a single list of contents for files stored to **Google Docs, Box.net and Dropbox**.

MANAGEMENT APPLICATIONS

There are apps available for management task such as **time tracking, organizing notes**. Applications performing such tasks are discussed below:

SN	Application Description
1	**Toggl** It helps in tracking time period assigned to a particular project.
2	**Evernote** Evernote is an application that organizes the sticky notes and even can read the text from images which helps the user to locate the notes easily.
3	**Outright** It is an accounting app. It helps to track income, expenses, profits and losses in real time.

SOCIAL APPLICATIONS

There are several social networking services providing websites such as Facebook, Twitter etc.

SN	Application Description
1	**Facebook** **Facebook** offer social networking service. One can share photos, videos, files, status and much more.
2	**Twitter** **Twitter** helps to interact directly with the public. Once can follow any celebrity, organization and any person who is on twitter and can have latest updates regarding the same.

ENTERTAINMENT APPLICATIONS

SN	Application Description
1	**Audiobox.fm** It offers streaming service i.e. music can be stored online and can be played from cloud using service's own media player.

ART APPLICATIONS

SN	Application Description
1	**Moo** It offers art services such as designing and printing **business cards, poscards** and **minicards.**

CLOUD PROVIDERS

Various Cloud Computing platforms are available today. The following table contains the popular Cloud Computing platforms:

SN	Platforms Description
1	**Salesforce.com** This is a Force.com development platfrom. This provide a simple user interface and lets users log in, build an app and push it in the cloud.
2	**Appistry** The Appistry's CloudQ platform is efficient in delivering a run-time application platform. This platform is very useful to create scalable and service oriented applications.
3	**AppScale** The AppScale is an open source platform for Google App Engine applications.
4	**AT&T** The AT&T allows access to virtual servers and manages the virtualization AT&T The AT&T allows access to virtual servers and manages the virtualization infrastructure. This virtualization infrastructure includes network, server and storage.

5 **Engine Yard**

The Engine Yard is a Rails Application cloud computing platform.

6 **Enomaly**

Enomaly's provides the Infrastructure-as-a-Service platform.

7 **FlexiScale**

The FlexiScale offers a cloud computing platform that allows flexible, scalable and automated cloud infrastructure.

8 **GCloud3**

The GCloud3 offers private cloud solution in its gPlatform.

9 **Gizmox**

The Gizmox Visual WebGUI platfrom is best suited for developing new web apps and modernize the legacy apps based on ASP.net, DHTML etc.

10 **GoGrid**

The GoGrid platform allows the users to deploy web and database cloud services.

11 **Google**

The Google's App Engine, let the users build, run and

maintain their applications on Google's infrastructure.

12 LongJump

The LongJump offers a Business Application Platform, a platform-as-a-Service (PaaS).

13 Microsoft

The Microsoft's Windows Azure is a cloud computing platform, offering an environment to create cloud apps and services.

14 OrangeScape

OrangeScape is offers a Platform-as-a-Service (Paas) for non programmers. Building an app is as easy as spreadsheet.

15 RackSpace

The RackSpace provide servers-on-demand via a cloud-driven platfrom of virtualized servers.

16 Amazon EC2

The Amazon EC2 (Elastic Compute Cloud) lets the users configure and control computing resources while running them on Amazon's environment.

CLOUD COMPUTING CHALLENGES

Cloud computing, an emergence technology, have placed many challenges in different aspects. Some of these are shown in the following diagram:

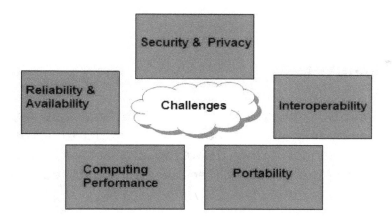

SECURITY & PRIVACY

Security and Privacy of information is the biggest challenge to cloud computing. To get out of security and privacy issues can be over come by employing encryption, security hardware and security applications.

PORTABILITY

This is another challenge to cloud computing that applications should easily be migrated form one cloud provider to another. There should not be vendor-lock in. However, it is not yet made possible because each of the cloud provider use different standard languages for their platforms.

INTEROPERABILITY

Application on one platform should be able to incorporate services from other platfrom. It is made possible via web services. But this writing such web services is very complex.

COMPUTING PERFORMANCE

To deliver data intensive applications on cloud requires high network bandwidth which result in high cost. If done at low bandwidth, then it does not meet the required computing performance of cloud application.

RELIABILITY AND AVAILABILITY

It is necessary for cloud systems to be reliable and robust because most of the business are now becoming dependent on services provided by third party.

MOBILE CLOUD COMPUTING

Cloud Computing offers such smartphones that have rich internet media experience and require less processing, less power. In term of Mobile Cloud Computing, processing is done in cloud, data is stored in cloud. And the mobile devices serve as a media for display.

Today smartphones are employed with rich cloud services by integrating applications that consume web services. These web services are deployed in cloud.

There are several Smartphone operating systems available such as **Google's Android, Apple's iOS, RIM BlackBerry, Symbian,** and **Windows Mobile Phone**. Each of these platform support third party applications that are deployed in cloud.

ARCHITECTURE

MCC includes four types of cloud resources:

- Distant mobile cloud
- Distant immobile cloud
- Proximate mobile computing entities
- Proximate immobile computing entities
- Hybrid

The following diagram shows the framework for mobile cloud computing architecture:

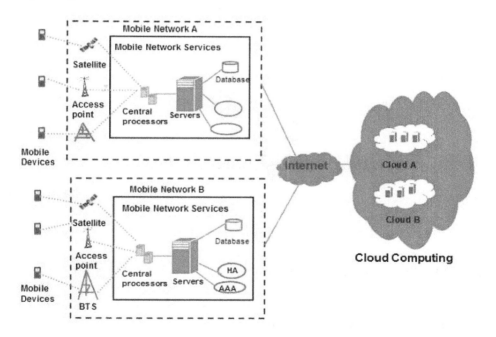

ISSUES

Despite of having significant development in field of mobile computing, there still exists many issues:

EMERGENCY EFFICIENT TRANSMISSION

There should be a frequent transmission of information between cloud and the mobile devices.

ARCHITECTURAL ISSUES

Mobile cloud computing is required to make architectural neutral because of heterogeneous environment.

LIVE VM MIGRATION

It is challenging to migrate an application which is resource-intensive to cloud and to execute it via. Virtual Machine .

MOBILE COMMUNICATION CONGESTION

Due to continuous increase demand for mobile cloud services, the workload to enable smooth communication between cloud and mobile devices has been increased.

SECURITY AND PRIVACY

This is one of the major issue because mobile users share their personal information over the cloud.